SMALL BUT DEADLY

Tom Jackson

D1081185

KENT
LIBRARIES & ARCHIVES
C153645031

Copyright © ticktock Entertainment Ltd 2008

First published in Great Britain in 2008 by ticktock Media Ltd,
2 Orchard Business Centre, North Farm Road, Tunbridge Wells, Kent, TN2 3XF

project editor: Ruth Owen
ticktock project designer: Sara Greasley
ticktock picture researcher: Lizzie Knowles

**With thanks to series editors Honor Head and Jean Coppendale,
and consultant Sally Morgan.**

Thank you to Lorraine Petersen and the members of nasen

ISBN 978 1 84696 745 0 pbk

Printed in China

A CIP catalogue record for this book is available from the British Library.
No part of this publication may be reproduced, copied, stored in a retrieval system or transmitted in any form or
by any means electronic, mechanical, photocopying, recording or otherwise without prior written permission of
the copyright owner.

Picture credits (t=top; b=bottom; c=centre; l=left; r=right):
Esther Beaton/Rex Features: 27. John Chapple/Rex Features: 26. Martin Dohrn/Science Photo Library: 5. Jurgen
Freund/Nature Picture Library: 6-7, 8. istock: 2-3, 10-11, 18. Mark Moffett/Minden Pictures/FLPA: 21, 22-23. A.N.T.
Photo Library/NHPA: 24. Jeffrey L. Rohman/Corbis: 17. Shutterstock: OFC, 1, 4, 7 (inset), 9, 12, 13, 14-15, 15t (inset)
19t, 19b, 28-29, 31. Volker Steger/Science Photo Library: 25. Birgitte Wilms/Minden Pictures/FLPA: 16.

Every effort has been made to trace copyright holders, and we apologise in advance for any omissions. We would be
pleased to insert the appropriate acknowledgments in any subsequent edition of this publication.

CONTENTS

SMALL BUT DEADLY

What would you prefer to meet –
a snarling tiger, or a tiny fly?
A great white shark or a snail?

Large, fierce animals can be dangerous.

However, some of the biggest killers on Earth...

...are smaller than a coin!

The tsetse fly from Africa lives by sucking blood from people and animals. As it does this, it spreads a disease.

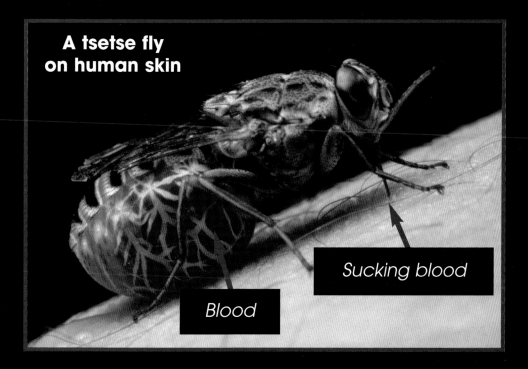

A tsetse fly on human skin

Sucking blood

Blood

The disease makes people fall asleep – and never wake up! It kills thousands of people each year.

The tsetse fly may be small...

...but it is deadly!

INVISIBLE KILLER

The most venomous animal on Earth is the box jellyfish. It lives in the Pacific Ocean.

The see-through box jellyfish is almost invisible.

Tentacles

The jellyfish's tentacles have millions of dart-shaped stingers. It fires the stingers into its victim. The stingers release venom into the victim.

*A scientist studies
a box jellyfish*

A box jellyfish's sting can kill a
person in less than four minutes.

Vinegar can save
your life!

**Vinegar stops the stings
from working.
Then they can be removed.**

TWO DAYS OF PAIN

The Irukandji jellyfish lives in the sea near Australia. Its sting doesn't kill, but it is so painful, its victims sometimes wish they were dead!

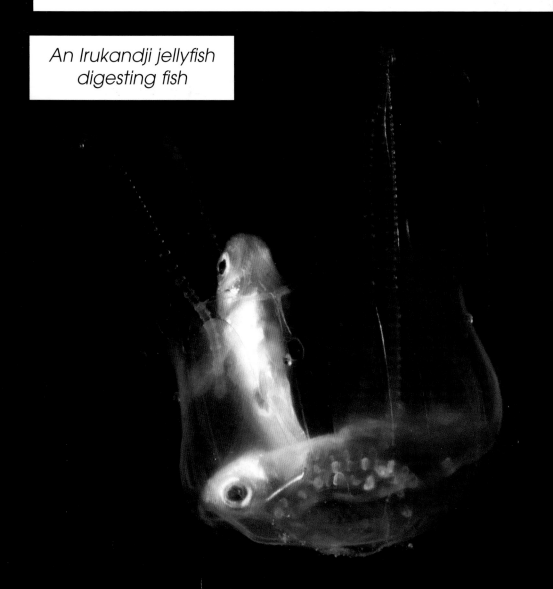

An Irukandji jellyfish digesting fish

This tiny jellyfish is only the size of your thumb.

The venom makes you ache, itch, sweat and twitch. You feel very sick and you are in agony.

The pain goes on for about...
...30 hours non-stop.

No one knows how the venom works.

A scientist was stung on purpose by an Irukandji jellyfish. He wanted to work out how the venom works. The scientist said:

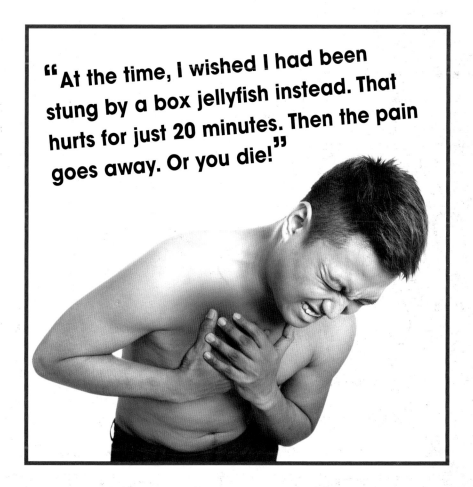

"At the time, I wished I had been stung by a box jellyfish instead. That hurts for just 20 minutes. Then the pain goes away. Or you die!"

POISON PUFFER

When in danger, pufferfish puff up into a round ball.
This makes it hard for a predator to bite them.

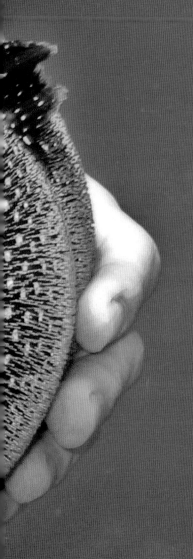

The pufferfish makes a strong, deadly poison inside its body.

The poison is stored in the fish's liver and skin.

If a person eats poisonous pufferfish flesh, it paralyses their muscles.

They can't breathe.

They suffocate to death!

ZOMBIE POISON

On the Caribbean Island of Haiti, some people believe pufferfish poison is used by sorcerers. They believe sorcerers use it to turn people into zombies - the walking dead!

Can someone really be turned into a zombie? Some scientists think they can explain this.

If a person was fed a small amount of pufferfish poison, it could paralyse them.

The person would not be able to move. Their heartbeat would almost stop.

The person would seem dead – even to a doctor.

The victim might even be buried in a grave.

But then the poison would wear off.
The person might climb out of their grave.

They would seem to be...

...the walking dead!

STONEFISH

The stonefish is one of the most venomous fish on Earth! It lurks among rocks on coral reefs.

If you tread on a stonefish, the spikes on its back jab into your foot. The spikes can even jab you through a shoe.

Coral reef

Stonefish

Venom squirts into your skin. The venom makes it hard for you to breathe.

Your foot will be in agony.

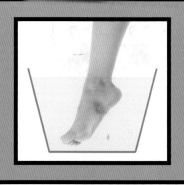

Put your foot in hot water to help the pain.

Go to a medical centre right away to get treatment.

The fish looks just like a stone!

BLUE RINGS FOR DANGER

The blue-ringed octopus grows no bigger than a golf ball – but it's still deadly!

The blue rings are a sign the octopus is about to attack.

If this octopus bites you, it will inject venom into your body.

The venom will make you blind.

It will paralyse you.

You will be dead in minutes.

The blue-ringed octopus is a popular pet in south-east Asia. However, many owners are accidentally killed by their deadly pets.

Blue-ringed octopus

In Thailand it is against the law to own a blue-ringed octopus. Owning one will get you six months in prison.

PIRANHAS

Piranhas are little fish with big teeth.
They live in rivers in South America.

One piranha can give a nasty bite.

But if piranhas gang together...

...they can be deadly!

Sometimes rivers start to dry up when it is hot. Lots of piranhas have to live together in a small amount of water.

Then, the piranhas hunt as a pack.

When a large animal, such as a cow, comes to drink – the piranhas attack!

Cow skull

The victim is stripped to its bones.

KILLER FROG

The golden poison dart frog is just 5 centimetres long. However, some scientists think it might have enough poison to kill ten people!

The poison comes from the ants and beetles the frog eats.

The poison works through the frog's skin.

Just touching the frog gives you a painful rash.

If a predator bites the frog, the predator will be dead in minutes!

The golden poison dart frog lives in the rainforests of Colombia in South America.

POISON ARROWS

Hunters in the rainforest use poison
from the golden poison dart frog
on their arrow tips.

The arrow tip is rubbed on the frog's skin.

Any animal struck by the arrow will be paralysed in seconds.

Arrow tip

DEADLY SNAILS

Dr Jon-Paul Bingham has a dangerous job. He milks snails! The snails are not garden snails. They are deadly cone shells that live in the sea.

Dr Bingham collects venom from the cone shells. He uses the venom to make new drugs, such as painkillers.

Breathing tube

Harpoon comes from here

Cone shells have a harpoon. They use it to spear fish.

Cone shells pump venom into their victim through the harpoon.

Harpoon seen through a microscope

They pump enough venom to kill 15 people!

If Dr Bingham gets stung, he will be in trouble.

His local hospital know to get him onto a life-support machine fast. If the machine can keep him alive, his body will clear out the venom.

A scientist milks the spider for its venom. It can be used to make an antidote.

DEADLY SPIDER

The Sydney funnel-web spider is one of the world's most venomous spiders. It lives in Australia.

The spider has a deadly bite. Its venom will make you sweat and vomit. It will also make you twitch – you won't be able to control it.

Within a few hours, you may die from a swollen brain.

However, there is an antidote to the venom. So get to a hospital fast!

Funnel-web spider in a pool filter

The spiders often fall into garden swimming pools. They can survive underwater for up to 24 hours.

WORLD'S BIGGEST KILLER

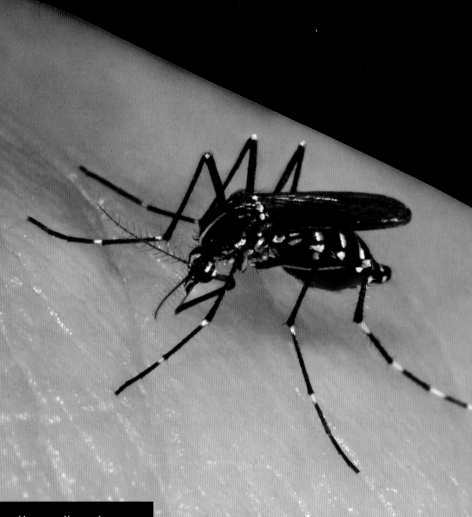

Mosquitoes live by sucking blood from people and animals.

The most dangerous animal on Earth is the tiny mosquito.

Every year, 70 million people catch diseases from mosquito bites.

When mosquitoes bite people, they spread deadly diseases such as malaria and yellow fever.

At least one million people die from malaria each year.

NEED TO KNOW WORDS

agony A terrible pain.

antidote A drug that stops a venom or poison killing a person.

coral reef A rocky area in warm, shallow seas. A coral reef is made of the chalky remains of huge numbers of tiny animals called coral polyps.

deadly Something that causes death.

harpoon A type of arrow or spear.

life-support machine A machine that keeps a seriously ill person alive. The machine does the work of the person's heart and lungs.

malaria A disease that causes liver and brain damage. It is most common in Africa and south-east Asia.

paralyse Made unable to move all or part of the body.

poison A substance that can kill or hurt a person or animal.

rainforest A jungle of tall trees that grows in hot, wet parts of the world.

sorcerer Someone who can make magic.

suffocate To die because you cannot breathe.

venom A poison that is deliberately passed onto a victim through a bite or sting.

venomous An animal that uses venom to kill prey or to defend itself.

victim A person or animal who is hurt or killed.

yellow fever A killer disease that causes the victim's skin to go yellow. Yellow fever is found in South America and Africa.

A DEADLY BEAN!

One of the deadliest living things is not an animal, but a bean!

- The castor bean contains a deadly poison called ricin. If pure ricin gets into your blood, it can kill you. A pellet of ricin the size of a pinhead could kill a person in hours.

- In 1978, Russian spies used ricin to kill a man named Ceorgi Markov. They fired a tiny pellet filled with ricin into Markov's leg. They used a mini airgun hidden in an umbrella!

Castor bean plant pods with beans growing inside.

READ MORE ONLINE

Websites

http://magma.nationalgeographic.com/ngexplorer/0603/games/game_intro.html

http://kids.nationalgeographic.com/Animals/CreatureFeature/Poison-dart-frog

http://www.barrierreefaustralia.com/the-great-barrier-reef/blueringedoctopus.htm

INDEX